Psychedelic
Christianity

Psychedelic Christianity

Jack Call

CHRISTIAN
ALTERNATIVE

Winchester, UK
Washington, USA

First published by Christian Alternative Books, 2018
Christian Alternative Books is an imprint of John Hunt Publishing Ltd.,
No. 3 East St., Alresford, Hampshire SO24 9EE, UK
office1@jhpbooks.net
www.johnhuntpublishing.com
www.christian-alternative.com

For distributor details and how to order please visit the 'Ordering' section on our website.

Text copyright: Jack Call 2017

ISBN: 978 1 78535 747 3
978 1 78535 748 0 (ebook)
Library of Congress Control Number: 2017942029

A CIP catalogue record for this book is available from the British Library.

Design: Stuart Davies

Printed and bound by CPI Group (UK) Ltd, Croydon, CR0 4YY, UK

We operate a distinctive and ethical publishing philosophy in all areas of our business, from our global network of authors to production and worldwide distribution.

Contents

Also by Jack Call
God is a Symbol of Something True
Dreams and Resurrection

Chapter One

What's the point?

In one of Woody Allen's films there is a flashback scene of the protagonist as a schoolboy announcing to his parents one day that he isn't going to go to school any more. "What's the point?" he asks. "We are all going to die anyway." (I'm quoting from memory, so the actual quote may be slightly different.) And Allen has said that he believes that there is no eternal life, that life is meaningless, and that the only purpose in his art of writing and making movies, the only purpose of anything in life, is to distract us momentarily from the bleak fact that there is no point to anything.

The fictional character Obermann, in Senancour's epistolary novel of the same name, said, "Man is perishable.... That may be, but let us perish resisting, and if annihilation must be our portion, let us not make it a just one." And Unamuno, who quotes Obermann approvingly, said that if we die utterly then humanism is a cruel joke. But suppose we don't die utterly. Suppose we die but are resurrected and have life everlasting. We can still imagine a schoolboy refusing to do his homework and asking, "What's the point since we all have everlasting life anyway?" One can grant that we all want to be something and not nothing and also recognize that just realizing that we can't go out of existence, while a joyous relief from anxiety about being sucked away into nothingness, is not enough to assure us that everything is fundamentally all right. We can still ask, "What is the point, the goal, the purpose? What is it all for?" Schelling remarked, "Being infinite is for itself not a perfection. It is rather the marker of that which is imperfect. The perfected is precisely the in itself full, concluded, finished." (p. 7, *The Ages of the World*) But when it is concluded, finished, is there nothing beyond that boundary? If there is something, what is it? If there isn't anything, aren't we back to anxiety about eventual nothingness? How can there be everlasting life *and* an end or goal or state of perfection that is the point of it all?

Is there an ultimate goal? If not, how can that be all right? If so, what is it? Could it be that there are different ultimate goals for different people? I don't mean just people having different beliefs about what the ultimate goal is. I mean: could it be that there really are different ultimate goals for different people, no matter what people may believe about that? We need to think about that word "ultimate." In one sense, it just means "the last." Might it turn out that each person's ultimate goal is just whatever goal he or she had last before dying, the goal of taking a deep breath, or the goal of saying "Help me!" for instance? We have many different goals throughout life. Whether a person's ultimate goal is just the last one she or he has before dying would depend, for one thing, on whether or not there is an afterlife. If, as I believe, there is, then the last one in life is not the last one of all.

But "ultimate" can also mean more than just the last item in a series. It can mean something that justifies in some sense everything that came before, or something like the supreme exemplar of a type of thing, as a resort might be claimed to be "the ultimate in luxury."

Could it be that the ultimate goal is simply to tell the truth? Jesus said, "And you shall know the truth, and the truth shall make you free." (John 8:32) That suggests that being free is the ultimate goal. And Jesus talked about knowing the truth, not telling the truth. In an essay on truth, Unamuno distinguished two concepts of truth. One is the truth that may or may not be known, that is, the objective facts about how things are. The other is the faithful correspondence between a person's inner states or processes of believing and what he or she communicates to someone else. It is the distinction between knowing the truth, or hoping to discover it, and telling the truth. The opposite of

2

knowing the truth is being ignorant. The opposite of telling the truth is lying. The outward evidence in both cases is the same: someone saying something false or otherwise acting as if something false is true. What distinguishes the two is an interior intent. This distinction is no great revelation, but it is often ignored when someone unfairly accuses someone else of lying who really just sincerely has a false belief and isn't guilty of being willfully ignorant. The interesting claim that Unamuno makes is that the moral concept of telling the truth is more fundamental than the non-moral concept of the truth as being correctly informed. The latter derives from the former. It's as if we want the world to give up its secrets and not mislead us just in the same way we want another person to tell us the truth and not lie to us. But does the world keep secrets from us and mislead us? It does inasmuch as the world includes people and sometimes non-human animals and even plants who do that. Surely it would be gross anthropomorphism to attribute deceitful intent to the inorganic parts of the world. And yet from our human, reactive side, we do resent the resistance of the inorganic parts of the world, too. I can be angry at a roof tile that falls on my head, and I can be angry in a similar way at an ignorant person who spreads misinformation. And that helps explain why we also unfairly accuse an ignorant person of deliberately telling a lie. Of course, I don't accuse someone of lying unless I know, or at least think I know, that what he or she says is false, in which case I am not being deceived. But I might have been deceived at first, before I discovered the truth; and anyway it is an insult to be lied to, even when the intent to deceive fails. Unamuno wrote:

> "The only perfect homage that can be rendered to God is the homage of truth. The kingdom of God, whose advent is mechanically exhorted every day by millions of tongues defiled by lies, is none other than the kingdom of truth." ("What is Truth?" *Selected Works of Unamuno, Vol. 5*, p. 168)

"But how can you tell the truth if you don't know what the truth is?" someone might ask. The objection would be that truth as the objective facts about how things are is more fundamental after all. But I think Unamuno is right. The reply is that if you don't know what the truth is about some particular claim, then the truth you should tell is that you don't know; but that there are plenty of things you do know from the inside, and it is heavenly when you are willing to tell the truth about them. You know enough. Telling the truth, faithfully communicating your thoughts as they are, is sufficiently demanding. If we all lived up to it, we would be in the kingdom of heaven. Or, we are in the kingdom of heaven, but we lie to each other that we aren't. Why do we do that? Why do I do that? I think what Jesus was saying was that he was telling the truth, for those who had ears to hear it, about what really matters, the ultimate goal.

Of course, not all religious believers call the ultimate goal "the kingdom of heaven." Hindus call it "moksha"; Buddhists, "nirvana." And not everyone is a religious believer. For a secular humanist, as I once considered myself to be, the ultimate goal is human well-being in the only life each of us has. The Epicureans call it "ataraxia," or not being disturbed, that is, a state of equanimity. The Stoics think it is the absence of unhealthy passions, and that it is the same thing as virtue. If there is an ultimate goal, these might be just different ways of trying to conceive of it or to say what it is. We all should tell the truth about what we think when we try to say whether there is an ultimate goal and if so, what it is.

I can see a reason for hoping there is no ultimate goal. That is that once the goal is achieved, if it was really the ultimate goal, then everything would be over and done. I suppose I could still do things, but none of them could be justified as necessary to reach the ultimate goal. This would be a reason for thinking that there can be goals that not only are not ultimate but that don't even contribute in any way to the ultimate goal. Should we say that until the ultimate goal is achieved, no other goal should be pursued except as a means to the ultimate goal; but once the ultimate goal has been attained, there can be other goals to be pursued simply for their own sake? This raises the question whether I hope there is just one ultimate goal, because if there can be more than one goal, each of which is to be pursued simply for its own sake, isn't that another way of saying that there are more ultimate goals than one? But doesn't "ultimate" imply uniqueness? Yes, but it could be that the uniqueness is only relative to the other non-ultimate goals which are to be pursued as a means to achieving it. We would pursue an ultimate goal by achieving subordinate goals which are necessary conditions for the achievement of that ultimate goal, which itself would not be a means to achieving any other goal but would be purely an end in itself. Once we have attained the ultimate goal, we then find that a new goal presents itself, and there would be various and sundry subordinate steps to be taken, each of which would be a means to reaching that new ultimate goal. But it would have to be that the attainment of the previous ultimate goal (ultimate in relation to the means required to achieve it) would not have been in its turn simply a first step towards the second ultimate goal we were supposing; because if it were, then the first one wouldn't have been an ultimate goal in its own right. In other words, if there are many ultimate goals, they must be equally and independently ultimate, with no other final goal that justifies each of them. Relative to each other, they would be neither ultimate nor subordinate, but each of them would be ultimate in relation to the subordinate goals that were the means of achieving it. But since we are supposing there is no other ultimate goal that would render any of them subordinate, each of them would be ultimate not only relative to the prior subordinate goals required to achieve it but also absolutely ultimate. Thus, we don't have to suppose that attaining the ultimate goal would mean that there is nothing more to do, because a new ultimate goal could be revealed that does not in any way render the ultimate goal already attained a mere means to the new ultimate goal, even though the past is always contained in the present. Thus an artist creates more than one work of art, two parents have more than one child, God creates each of us, and it is possible to have more than one peak psychedelic experience.

If I've already achieved the goal, then there is no point in seeking it. If I have a new goal, I can seek that. What do I hope about whether or not there is an ultimate goal and what do I hope about what it might be? Is the goal to be free of suffering? If I am suffering intensely, the answer will seem to be Yes. But to be freed of suffering is too negative a goal, implying that it would be best of all if I had never been born in the first place, since that is the only sure guarantee of never suffering. I know I don't want that to be true, and I don't know of any good reason to believe it is. But please, dear God, don't put me to the test! I want there to be something that is worth suffering for, without making the suffering itself the goal. I want the goal to involve cessation of any suffering that was necessary to achieve it but also to have a joyful, positive content that then makes any suffering on the way to it simply irrelevant. That is, I want it to be so that it would have been just fine if I had achieved it without going through any suffering but also just fine that in fact I had to go through suffering to attain it.

Eternity, timelessness, is not what I want. I want the right amount of stability and predictability, but I also want absolutely fresh newness, as on the day of Creation, with solids that look like they have just gelled from liquid, and liquids that look like shining solids, and everything breathing and squirming with life; and that requires what Bergson called "la durée," duration, our lived time of constant new creation, for even if something is repeated, the repetition is not the original. Now, you could say that if it is always the present containing the past and generating a genuinely new world, then that is what is eternally happening.

Always = eternally. The eternity that scares me is the eternity of absolute stillness, of nothing new, of everything being over and done with and just there, frozen, motionless, stale and suffocating. That is what Bergson identifies as the mistake of conceiving of time as the same thing as space.

I want to be able to change without the change ever being that I no longer exist. And I want the change to be enjoyable, or if not enjoyable, then leading to some further change that redeems it. And when I say "change," I mean something that has never occurred before in just that way. I'm not ruling out recognizable patterns and repetitions. In fact, I want those too! And I want it all ultimately to be humanly meaningful, neither entirely comprehensible (because that would mean it was over and done) nor intellectually repugnant (because that would mean I don't know what I mean), but morally and emotionally satisfying, and sensually and intellectually beautiful. And I don't want this just for myself but for everyone. If life is ultimately meaningless suffering or pleasure – I don't believe there is such a thing as meaningless joy – for even one person, then it is for me too, and I have missed the ultimate goal. It follows that if even one person achieves the ultimate goal, then everyone does. This, I believe, is the essence of Christianity. It is also, I think, what Unamuno meant by the phrase "the human finality of the universe."

Chapter Two

Finality

Nietzsche said that the only real affirmation of life would be a willingness to live it over again just as it was. But that claim is paradoxical, because living it over again just as it was would require that one not be conscious that it was being repeated, since otherwise it wouldn't be subjectively just as it was. So, the possibility one would be willing to undergo would be no different subjectively from having lived one's life just one time and not ever again. What seems right about his thought is that an affirmation of life as one has known it can't appeal to an as yet unexperienced, dramatically different kind of life that would compensate for the inadequacies of life as one has known it, for that is to express a dissatisfaction with life as one has known it. But why can't one affirm life as one has known it to be, believing, "Yes, I am glad I have had my life just as it has been, and when I have to leave this life behind, I would be happy to have another one of the same kind," and yet also hope it could be even better?

In *Dreams and Resurrection* I tried to explain why I think the wiping out of one's own subjectivity forever is not a real possibility. That helps tremendously when facing dying and death, but having lived through the dying of some important people in my life recently, I've been thinking that the ultimate goal that I hope for includes not only the assurance of everlasting life but also something that guarantees that the suffering that is the inevitable decline into death, that eventually occurs in each life before or as a new life begins, is compensated by some ultimate ongoing glorious joy. In that previous work I stated that it is reasonable to expect the next life to be very similar to this one, with its own joys and sorrows, deaths of loved ones and one's own death to be faced, with no death final but always

8

life after life. Now I'm saying I also hope that there is that human finality of the universe as I've tried to describe above that guarantees the meaningfulness and joy of the unending series. And I'm thinking that there is something unsatisfactory about the idea of an unending series. Or rather, it is all right for there to be an unending series, but there also needs to be something that is not an unending series. And it can't be the finality of eternal death, which would certainly be no solution since its nothingness, if it were really possible, would be just as unending. As Santayana said, "There is something baffling about infinity; in its presence the sense of finite humility can never wholly banish the rebellious suspicion that we are being deluded." (*The Sense of Beauty*, p. 64) And Schelling had one of the characters in his *Clara, or On Nature's Connection to the Spirit World*, say the following:

> "What is completed is generally more excellent and magnificent than infinity; in art it is the very seal of perfection. However, this universe is the most excellent of all, not only in itself but also as the work of a divine artist, and I asked him if he wouldn't have done better to have tackled the matter from this side than with general concepts, and whether he shouldn't have asked his opponent which was the most perfect, an infinite row of worlds, an eternal circle of beings without a final goal of perfection, or a universe that amounted to something definite or perfect." (p. 70)

Since the universe comprises everything that has ever existed, now exists, or will exist in the future, it includes every instance of anything that is completed and perfect. The question is whether the universe itself is or ever will be complete and perfect. Another way of putting the question is to ask whether it is better that there be many independently ultimate goals, as I outlined above, or instead that there be only one truly ultimate goal.

Kant said we should always treat humanity as an end in itself and never only as a means. I understand this to mean that it is all right to treat someone as a means to an end, as long as we also treat him or her as an end in himself or herself. An example is the employer/employee relation. The employer treats the employee as a means to producing the product or service which is sold for a profit to enhance the material prosperity of the employer. And the employee treats the employer as a means to improving his or her own material well-being. This is all right as long as each of them also recognizes the humanity of the other as an end in itself, which means thinking and acting so that the other's interests as a subject take priority over the use of him or her as an object. One should never act on the principle, "I don't care what you want as long as I get you to act in such a way that I get what I want," but it is all right to act on the principle, "I will try to get you to act in such a way that I get what I want unless this involves treating you as if your getting what you want is not just as important to you as my getting what I want is to me." Best of all, of course, is when what one person wants to have done for him or her is exactly what the other person wants to do.

Now suppose that there is only one ultimate goal. Wouldn't it be the case that even though there could be other goals which would be ends in themselves, they would also be correctly seen as at best mere means to the one ultimate goal? In which case, the maxim would be always to treat everything other than the one ultimate goal as a means to that ultimate goal and never only as an end in itself. Is everyone to be treated as just as ultimate an end as there can be, in which case there are as many ultimate ends as individual subjects of experience; or, is there one ultimate end that is more important even than the lesser ends that are all the individual subjects?

I think we have to choose the former alternative, because unless there is a subject who experiences the one ultimate end, it would not be of any worth to anyone. Suppose the subject who experiences the one ultimate end is God. But if we don't somehow take part in God's enjoyment of the ultimate end, then it doesn't really concern us, and he isn't really our God. So, each of us is an ultimate end in herself or himself, in that we must be there to take part in the joy of the achievement or gift of the ultimate end. (1 Corinthians 15:20-28)

It makes as little sense to try to separate one's continued existence from the ultimate goal by thinking of it as a mere means to the ultimate goal as it does to try to imagine the supremely desirable, the pearl of great price, as separate from the enjoyment of it. But it doesn't follow that one's mere continued existence, without regard to whether one ever enjoys the ultimate goal, is an ultimate end in itself. This leads us back again to the question of what the ultimate goal is and whether it is reasonable to hope to attain it.

Aristotle attempted to answer the question of what happiness is, in his *Nicomachean Ethics,* and said that it is acting in accordance with virtue, and if there is more than one virtue, then with the highest virtue. He didn't ignore the fact that we are social beings, and he wrote about the importance of friendship. He ended by identifying a life of philosophic contemplation as the highest form of happiness of which humans are capable. But since we are mortal, only the eternal God will always be thinking about thinking. I agree with Pascal and Unamuno. The eternal existence of a being who is thinking about thinking is not what I hope the ultimate goal is.

Plato represented Socrates as believing in immortality in the form of the continued existence of an immaterial soul, which may become embodied again but is only truly liberated and happy when it exists without a body. This is very similar to the Hindu concept of reincarnation, with *moksha,* the final liberation, being an escape from the cycle of deaths and rebirths and the recognition that one was really the only ultimate reality, Brahman, all along. The problem I have with Plato's vision is that it isn't clear to me how one can continue to be oneself without a body. The problem with the Hindu view is that one doesn't continue to be oneself in the sense in which one is a unique person different from other people. Buddhism makes this even clearer by teaching that one never really was a separate self in the first place, and nirvana is realizing that fact in the deepest, most experiential, as opposed to merely intellectual, way. But no one is there who has the experience. There is just the experiencing.

In contrast, in Christianity and Islam one's own very personal self is who is either rewarded or punished in the afterlife; that hoped-for reward is the one and only ultimate goal and that dreaded punishment is the ultimate failure to achieve it. My understanding is that Judaism is ambivalent about whether or not there is such an afterlife, but that at any rate the ultimate goal is the complete fulfillment of the covenant of the Jewish people with Him whose very name is too sacred to be uttered.

I don't claim to be an expert on the world's religions. As a Protestant Christian, I believe there are no experts on religion in the relevant sense, or that we are all equally experts. By "relevant" I mean relevant to the question of whether there is an ultimate goal, or maybe more than one, and if so, what it is (or they are). I don't mean the question of what various religious traditions say about this. On that question, there are experts, and I am just an educated amateur. But speaking from my own tradition, as a Protestant Christian, I think each of us is entitled to say what he or she thinks the true message of Christianity is concerning the ultimate goal or goals, and to try to persuade the others. I am not saying I intend what I have to say only for an audience of fellow Christians. I am just confessing my limitations when it comes to understanding what other religious traditions teach about the ultimate goal or goals. I think I have reasons for preferring the message of Christianity to those of other religions I've read about, beyond just the fact that historically Christianity has been the dominant religion of the culture into which I was born; but I reserve the right to change my mind about that, and if I ever do find that I don't have good reasons for preferring the message of Christianity, I feel confident I won't hesitate to embrace instead the view that would then seem to me closer to the truth, since I have done this in the past. Whether this makes me less or more entitled to call myself a Christian, or less or more entitled to consider myself a philosopher, is up to you to decide for yourself. Do I care what you think? I wouldn't be writing this if I didn't.

Somewhere in Schelling's writings he remarked that he didn't see why a particular drop of water that had become part of the ocean couldn't still continue to be that particular drop. And in *Bruno, or On the Natural and the Divine Principle of Things,* he writes of the identity of the finite and the infinite: "And the self consists in this way of being, at one and the same time, subjective and objective, or infinite and finite." (p. 187) Here is my attempt at understanding this: My existence as a subject is infinite. When I think of a limit to myself, in time or space, I am thinking of myself as an object. Objectively, there was a time before I was born and there will be a time after I die. Objectively, I take up only a certain volume of space; and, although I can move through space, I can occupy only one place at a time. Further, there are practical limits on which spaces I can occupy while remaining alive. It is very different when I think of myself as the subject of all my thoughts and experiences. Subjectively, I cannot imagine a time before I was born or after I die, without lurking there somehow as an undetected subject; and I can't imagine any place, whether the one I occupy, one I could occupy but don't, or one I couldn't possibly practically occupy (e.g., in the interior of the sun), without being the subject of that imagination. That is what I understand by Schelling's identification of the subjective with the infinite, and the objective with the finite. And what he calls "the identity of the infinite and the finite" is the fact that I myself have a subjective side and an objective side and that they are sides of one and the same self. [Disclaimer: I also don't claim to be a Schelling scholar. It could be that other writings of Schelling show this was not his considered view, or that I am misinterpreting him even here, or that he would vehemently disagree with what I go on to say. I don't think so, or else I wouldn't feel good about appropriating his words, but my topic is more "how does what I read in Schelling stimulate my own thinking?" than it is "what did Schelling really mean?" I confess I don't feel confident about answering that last question, which would require more extended study of his works and commentary on them than I have accomplished so far.] This seems right to me, for which reason I find that I prefer the Christian and Islamic emphasis on one's own ultimate salvation or damnation to the Hindu and Buddhist transcendence of the self into a Self with a capital S (Hinduism) or a no-self at all (Buddhism). The Christian and Islamist view keeps both the finite and the infinite, the objective and the subjective, while the Hindu and Buddhist views see the ultimate goal as an annihilation of the objective finite in favor of the subjective infinite. The drop of water absorbed into the ocean is no more. There is only the ocean. There is only the dream of the ocean, and somehow there is not even a dreamer of this dream of the ocean.

I am aware that there are dualistic versions of Hinduism that share my objections to the non-dualistic (Advaita) Vedanta philosophy of Hinduism, and that there are Christian and Islamic mystics who long for self-annihilation, so let me be clear that I side with dualistic Hinduism and the more standard versions of Christianity and Islam on the question of whether it is desirable for one's own self to have everlasting life. That is: it is. Aside from reasons of cultural heritage, the reason I am a Christian rather than a Muslim is because I think the paradox asserted in Christianity that Jesus is both fully human and fully divine is more spiritually fruitful than the Islamic wavering between the denial that he was divine, which is justified on the grounds that this is to revert to polytheism or a pagan conception of God as someone who can have a son (4:171), and the denial that he was actually crucified, which seems to be a remnant of Docetism, an early Christian heresy, in the Qur'an, i.e., the view that Jesus only appeared to be human. (4:157)

Chapter Three

Monism, dualism, and the number of ultimate goals

There seems to be a strong prejudice in favor of monism over dualism or any other pluralism on the part of those who like to think of themselves as defenders of rationality against superstition. The kind of dualism I've come to accept is a dualism of subject and object or person and thing. I can't convince myself of either monistic alternative: (1) that ultimately there are only subjective points of view or (2) that ultimately there are only objects with no subjective points of view. Neither can I convince myself of nihilism, that ultimately there is nothing. But a first-person perspective of an objective state of affairs doesn't require one to deny that the object of experience is also there. It's like saying that every coin has two sides. Is that dualistic? It is, I suppose, in that it insists on the two sides, but since they are two sides of one and the same coin, it could also be called monistic or non-dualistic. On the other hand, any attempt to simplify by wiping out one of the sides – as in the philosophies of materialism (or physicalism) or subjective idealism (or phenomenalism), or in the religious views of Advaita Vedanta, the no-self doctrine of Buddhism, or Christian and Sufi mystical longings for self-annihilation – would be like insisting that the real coin has only one side.

There is real wisdom, I think, in the Christian doctrine of the resurrection of the body, which is also a form of mysticism. Life without a body would be so radically different from the life we have known that it isn't clear whether it would be desirable or not. I'm inclined to think that it wouldn't be. Each of us has known since childhood that he or she has life in a body that is going to die. It doesn't follow that the blankness of non-existence is our ultimate fate. In fact, as I argued in *Dreams and Resurrection,* it is an illusion that one's own subjective annihilation is a real possibility. But then if my body is going to die, but I will continue to exist as a subject of experience, doesn't it follow that I will be a disembodied spirit? No, that is only one hard-to-understand and not very desirable possibility. Easier to understand and more desirable is that my dead body will either come back to life or won't really be dead after all, or else I will have a new body, whether or not I will know it is new. (2 Corinthians 5:17) It is life I want and not floating in silent, invisible, odorless, tasteless, intangible space forever, thinking about thinking.

So, I don't think the ultimate goal requires the annihilation of me or anyone else. It will require my and your transformation, though, unless we think we have already attained it. Have we? And if not, what kind of transformation will it be?

I don't claim to know the answers to those questions, but I do have beliefs concerning them, based on religious experiences. One might think that the answer to the first question, at least, is obvious. Of course we haven't already attained the ultimate goal! If we had, we would know it, and we wouldn't need to ask or ponder about any of this. But isn't it possible that we have forgotten that we have already attained the ultimate goal; or, as I mentioned above, that there are a plurality of ultimate goals so that even though we have already attained one or more and wouldn't really need to do anything else, we are pleased to pursue a new one; or, that the ultimate goal just is to live this kind of life we are living, with its doubts, sufferings, and confusions, but also with its faith, joys, and clear insights? Regarding this question and the second question about the kind of transformation that occurs in attaining the ultimate goal, my two guiding stars are psychedelic experience and Christianity. Neither one shines brighter than the other, and so you shouldn't take the order in which I listed them or the length to which I will discuss each of them as any indication of a priority of one over

17

the other.

It is because I have had several profound psychedelic experiences that I hold open the possibilities that we have already attained the ultimate goal, that there may be more than one, and that there is and always will be another one coming. And Christianity, more than any other philosophy or religion that I know about, encourages me in the faith that these are not mere possibilities but are in fact the way things are.

* * *

We have already attained the ultimate goal. How so? What ultimate goal? Being in the right relationship with God. Mystics have always said that the experience of this cannot be conveyed in words, and the availability of LSD and other psychedelics hasn't changed that. But I now think "being in the right relationship with God" is as good a way as any to try to say what the ultimate goal is that is achieved in a peak psychedelic experience, which is, to say the least, the most intense kind of mystical experience I have had. I'm not denying that other people may have had just as intense mystical experiences some other way. I do deny the experiences could be any more intense. But how does the fact that one person, at a particular time or times, has experienced being in the right relationship with God imply that we have all attained this ultimate goal? It's a matter of seeing that being in the right relationship with God is always there, underlying everything else that could be described as *not* being in the right relationship with God. But this isn't a matter of knowing in the sense of propositional knowledge, that is, knowing that such and such is true; because even though the experience validates itself, it can't validate how one conceptualizes it. But it doesn't follow that there can't be reasons for preferring some ways of conceiving of it over others. Metaphysics and theology are noble pursuits in which it is difficult to be sure one is getting it mostly right, and the stakes are very high. That's why I don't insist at all on the verbal formula of "being in the right relationship with God" as the only proper verbal expression for what peaking on LSD, for example, is like. According to Huston Smith, the one positive characterization the Buddha would give of nirvana was to say that it is "bliss, pure bliss." That's fine, too. I just prefer Christian terminology like "the kingdom of God," "the kingdom of heaven," "being in the right relationship with God," for reasons I have mentioned and will continue to try to explain.

And what does Christianity say about whether we have already attained the ultimate goal? How can we look forward to the coming of the kingdom of God if it has already come? And yet Paul does seem to say both that we already have it and that it is still coming. As Rudolf Bultmann puts it, "To be sure, Paul still expected the end of the world as a cosmic drama, the *parousia* of Christ on the clouds of heaven, the resurrection from the dead, the final judgment, but with the resurrection of Christ the decisive event has already happened." (*Jesus Christ and Mythology,* p. 32) We are already no longer slaves but heirs to the kingdom. (Gal. 4:7) "So if anyone is in Christ, there is a new creation; everything old has passed away; see, everything has become new!" (2 Cor. 5:17) And the third chapter of the Gospel According to John makes this clear also. Whoever believes in the Son already has eternal life. And in the second chapter of his first letter he says that "the darkness is passing away and the true light is already shining." (1 John 2:8)

Now Paul and John also say that those who don't believe will endure God's wrath, and this seems to imply that not all of us have already attained the ultimate goal or ever will. But Paul also says that in the final culmination God will be all in all. (1 Cor. 15:28) In Acts 3:17-26 Peter is quoted as saying that God had announced the universal restoration long ago through the holy prophets. And Jesus himself speaks of the renewal of all things in Matt. 19:28. Now, I realize that not all Christians believe that ultimately everyone is saved, but I don't see how God can be all in all and restore all things if there are some people who are eternally suffering due to their rejection of and hence separation from God. That is why I believe that if anyone has really attained the ultimate goal, then everyone has. The worst thing that can happen is to suffer horror in the present and to dread that it will be everlasting or to believe that it cannot possibly be cancelled by something good.

* * *

There may be more than one ultimate goal. If we have already attained the ultimate goal, whether we remember having done so or not, why are we still here? What are we supposed to do with the rest of our lives? These are not questions one would ask while the process of ecstasy is ongoing, but part of being in the right relationship with God is realizing that one can stand only so much ecstatic bliss. I can only speak for myself, but I don't think I'm an exceptional case among those who are fortunate enough to have been around when taking a psychedelic trip was a thing much talked about in mostly positive terms (May such a time return! And to some degree it seems to be happening: Hooray!), so that I tried it, with a good set and setting, got into the right relationship with God (although I wouldn't have used such language at the time), and within a few weeks wanted to repeat the experiment. I don't think any of my subsequent trips were any more fun than that first one, but some were bigger, and some were at least partly hellish. Two in particular were so big that no words, no image, no thought would be an exaggeration of how important they were. But since each of these big trips was like a lifetime in itself – and two different lifetimes, although I was, am, and will be the one who came down from both of them – there is a sense in which it wasn't the same ultimate goal, the same way of being in the right relationship with God, in both of them, but rather two different but complementary ultimate goals. Neither required the other, and neither excluded the other. They both just happened, were accomplished, were given. But back to the way in which I don't think I'm exceptional. Gradually, I became less and less inclined to want to take a psychedelic trip. So there are limits to that method, as there are to all methods; but within those limits, paradoxically, the unlimited! Which is why I now prefer to call the ultimate goal being in the right relationship to God. My limits define me. Sometimes I like for them to come close to dissolving, but not most of the time.

In *The Ages of the World* Schelling wrote, "Everything can be communicated to the creature except for one thing. The creature cannot have the immortal ground of life in itself. The creature cannot be of and through itself." (p. 107) There are important things that I care about very much that are not under my control. I am glad I was born, but I didn't cause myself to be born – at least not in any way I can grasp. I just find myself here, alive, and it seems like it's always been this way, even though objectively there was a time before I was born into this world. Likewise, there will be a time when I will die in this world. Although I could cause myself to die, by committing suicide, I cannot cause myself not to die, and I can't cause myself to have an afterlife. But I believe that I will die, since that will just be the continuation of the well-established pattern of living things dying, and that I will have an afterlife, since I think the nothingness of eternal death is not a real possibility. Have I just agreed with Schilling or disagreed with him? Maybe a little of both.

God will be all in all. All things will be restored. What I hope this means is that I will still be who I am, you will still be who you are, and likewise for everybody else, but at the same time God will be in us and we will be in God, so that all suffering, all crime, all horror, all evil will be dissolved in a way that is experienced by each and every one of us as profound contentment. This is one ultimate goal, but it is also more than one, because the experience of it by each person will be just as ultimate as the experience of it by any other. This is my understanding of the parable of the lost sheep. The good shepherd leaves the ninety-nine and goes in search of the lost one because the lost one by itself is of just as ultimate value as any of the others, and these ultimate values don't sum up into one even more ultimate value. Each one is as ultimate as it gets.

And here is the flaw of utilitarian ethics: the assumption that there can be an impersonal, objective summing up of the values or disvalues of many subjective experiences, expressed in the slogan "the greatest happiness for the greatest number." A utilitarian shepherd would not risk losing a greater number of the ninety-nine sheep who haven't strayed by abandoning them in hopes of finding and saving the one sheep who strayed and got lost. The utilitarian high priest Caiaphas reasoned that it would be better to sacrifice the one man Jesus whom the Romans would perceive as threatening their authority than to risk Roman wrath against the rest of the Jews. (John 11:50) If we make the distinction between *the world,* that is, as objectively described from a hypothetical impersonal point of view, and *the kingdom of heaven,* which is this world as experienced in the only way it is ever experienced, that is, from the point of view of some particular subject of experience; then utilitarian ethics is the only rational method for deciding policy in the world, but it makes no sense in the kingdom of heaven.

If we make the subject of experience into an object of thought, then it is not also the subject of that thought of which it is the object. And so on. So, there is a way in which the subject of experience always eludes its conceptualization. But the object of experience is also elusive. While we try to pin it down, experience goes on and reveals more about it that we just left out, and so on. Nevertheless, I think I understand the distinction between subject and object and that experiencing always involves both, or, at least, is never purely subjective or purely objective. From my point of view, there are many other possible or actual points of view. The actual ones are the ones someone is actually enjoying or suffering. The possible ones are the ones someone could enjoy or suffer. The ultimate goal from my point of view is deep contentment from every possible or actual point of view.

* * *

There is and always will be another ultimate goal coming. Think of the difference between a drowsy consciousness of your surroundings in a dim room and a wide-awake awareness of what's there in a well-lit room or outside in the sunshine. You can imagine a gradual or a sudden transition from being drowsy to being fully awake and alert, and you can imagine sudden shifts or discrete levels in the transition to the well-lit, wide-awake condition. My memory of one of the two big trips I mentioned before is of an experience that was something like that, but what would correspond to the initial drowsy state was already one of being fully awake and alert in the ordinary way and what would correspond to the well-lit, fully awake condition was a tremendously more well-lit, fully awake, richly articulated super-consciousness of sights, sounds emotions, and bodily sensations that would reach a peak that was the utter fulfillment of everything that had gone before, so that everything was coming to an end, followed immediately by a new step up, a new turning up of the lights and a new culmination, and another, and another, which eventually began to descend a little at a time – but measurements of time were hard to grasp – and at every moment I was also fully aware of my surroundings as much as I ever was, the super-consciousness superimposed on the ordinary consciousness, until eventually I found myself worn out and amazed, with rest and sleep beginning to seem like actual possibilities. This is the way in which psychedelic experience has shown that one can reach the ultimate goal, as ultimate as one could have ever imagined or wished for, only to find the process immediately commencing and being fulfilled again in a completely new way, until one is eventually returned to a condition of remembering that this has happened and expecting it to happen again at some time in the future in a completely new way.

I don't expect that completely new way to involve my taking LSD or some other psychedelic again. There are limits to how many times one wants to pull off that kind of relaxation at the point of highest tension. The latest trend I've been reading about is microdosing, and that might be an easier way for more people to adjust to the existence of these mind-manifesting or God-inducing molecules.

The truth has already been revealed. It can be forgotten, ignored, seem to be hidden. But it is not hidden. It will be revealed again when it seems most hidden. That is the message of psychedelic experience, and it is the message of Christianity. We are still hoping, and we have good reason to hope, for the ultimate goal, when God will be all in all, and all things will be restored to an original state of glory. But the attainment of that ultimate goal will not mean we will be floating bodiless thoughts stuck in a suffocating loop of stale repetition. There will be a new ultimate goal, and we will have achieved everything that needed to be achieved.

Chapter Four

What Now?

So what do we do now? Or perhaps each of us should ask: What do I do now? Because we can work together or we can work independently. But maybe the word "work" is premature. We also play. One might think that identifying the ultimate goal would help one answer the question, "What do I do in light of that goal?" But given the choices open to me here and now in my particular circumstances, it is far from obvious which decisions I can make, which actions I can take, on my own or in cooperation with others, to help bring about the restoration of all things so that God will be all in all. I'm not God, and I can't control God, but it doesn't seem right that what I do makes no difference to whether or not the ultimate goal is achieved. Since the goal is for God to be all in all, then, since I'm just as much "all" as anybody else, it must be my goal as well as God's and everybody else's. And I don't know of any other goal of mine where what I do makes no difference to whether or not it is achieved. Even people who don't believe there is an ultimate goal manage to answer the question, "What should I do now?" in some way or other. Woody Allen, for example, who professes to believe that life is meaningless, decides to pursue his art of making movies in order to distract himself, he says, from the fact that life is meaningless. But what should I do, given what I believe about the ultimate goal?

One way to tackle this question is to ask first, "What am I doing?" and then ask, "Should I be doing something else instead?" In my own case, at the moment, I am writing this essay. Should I be doing something else? No, I don't think so. But as soon as I finished writing that last sentence, something happened so that I was distracted (My wife arrived home from grocery shopping, and I needed to help her bring things in), and then other things, and it is now the following day. Between the kinds of turning points or culminating experiences like the two big psychedelic trips I've mentioned, our lives are mostly like this, earning our daily bread, adding a new small piece to a larger project, preparing and eating meals, cleaning up, running errands, completing chores, resting, day-dreaming, sleeping and dreaming, and waking up to start again. And, as this life is an afterlife to a previous life, it is likely the afterlife will be like this, too. And since it includes litterbugs; robocallers; self-righteous hypocrites; minor aches and pains; bad trips; illnesses that make everything annoying and depressing; anxiety about injury, disease, and death; seeing people you love becoming physically and psychologically weaker and weaker until they die; finding out that someone you love has died suddenly and unexpectedly; as well as the sheer joy of being alive, loving and being loved, seeing colors, smelling aromas, tasting flavors, hearing musical sounds, interacting with charming and lovable people; it can seem as though we just get glimpses of a condition that could be described as God being all in all. I'm not complaining. Whenever I get such a glimpse, I can see that it doesn't matter that it's just a glimpse. What matters is the reality of what is glimpsed. But I'm not sure that answers the question of what I should do now, both on my own and in concert with other people. I don't think it really suggests that it doesn't matter what I do, since the pure goodness of it has to do with everything I care about the most.

In the early years after psychedelics had first burst upon the scene, the answer seemed simpler. Just spread the word, soon everyone would accept the "gratuitous grace" (Aldous Huxley), and peace and harmony would prevail. And you could tap into that deep well of religious experience again whenever you wanted, just by taking another trip. As it has turned out, society still has indigestion when it comes to psychedelics, one's next trip seems to be on indefinite hold, and the past, as always, is nothing more than what has led up to and is contained in the present. But that in no way invalidates the claims that psychedelic experience is religious experience and that it is or at least could be available at any time.

Similarly, in the early days of Christianity the miraculous was fresh in the memories of Jesus' followers and ongoing in their lives. His expected return was felt as imminent. But now twenty centuries have flashed by, the healings and raisings from the dead performed by Jesus, his own resurrection and ascension into heaven, and the heroics of the early saints seem more like old stories than fresh news, and the imminent transformation expected so long ago still hasn't happened, or if it has, it isn't in the way it seems that early Christians expected. But this doesn't invalidate the Christian claims of victory over sin and death and the ultimate restoration of all things so that God will be all in all.

Neither psychedelic experience nor Christianity can be relegated to the past. This is not a "post-Christian" era, and I am not an "aging hippie." From first to last breath in this life, we are all aging and facing something new, and that is a good thing. It means we are learning in the only way anybody ever learns anything. Psychedelic Christianity is as fresh as the tender shoots of spring. A psychedelic Christian is just a Christian who acknowledges that psychedelic experience is a way of learning how to be in the right relationship to God.

Chapter Five

God and control

In a previous work, I wrote that God is a symbol of the fact that there are important things that we care about very much that are beyond our control, either individually or collectively. A star example is whether or not one is loved. A friend of mine remarked, "Well, I think God is more than a symbol." But I don't mean God is a mere symbol, as a disappointed romantic might think he had discovered that love is just a word. I mean something more like the first line of the Tao Te Ching, which says that the Tao that can be named is not the Tao. I mean that believing in God is believing that there are important things, being born, for example, being loved, having to die, that are important to you but not under your control and that what makes it believing in God rather than the Devil, say, or just an indifferent universe, is that you cannot really be indifferent in return, and that you can learn or build up or have revealed to you a trust that overcomes the fear. One of Pascal's thoughts comes to mind: "Fear not, provided you are afraid. But if you are not afraid, be fearful." (p. 141)

Whether or not something is under one's control is even a mark to distinguish between fancy, or mere imagination, and reality. There is a sense in which anything I can imagine is real. That act of imagination is really part of my mental history. But we also contrast the imaginary with the real in the following way. I can change what I imagine at will. I can first imagine it one way and then another. That's all under my control. No matter what the weather outside, I can imagine warm sunshine and a fresh ocean breeze. But what I can't control is beyond the boundary of my imagination. I look out the window and see solid grey sky, and I think, "Though I can imagine the sky being blue right now, in reality it is grey."

There is an added complication when we consider dreams. In a dream it can seem that there are things that are outside of my control every bit as much as when I am awake. I don't typically believe, while I am dreaming, that I am just imagining everything that appears to be happening. But when I wake up and realize that I was just dreaming, I no longer attribute a reality, external to my mind, to those things that seemed not to be under my control while I was dreaming. So, in distinguishing between the reality I attribute to things when I am awake and the seeming reality of a dream, I am making a distinction between something that is really outside my control and something that only appeared, in the dream, to be outside my control. Of course, even when I realize it was a dream, I don't conclude that what I dreamed was under my conscious control, but I do typically dismiss the reasoning that because it was outside my conscious control, it was independently real as opposed to being a product of my mind.

There are borderline cases where it would be difficult to say definitively whether I am awake or asleep, where I might have the realization, "Oh, this is all really under my control." And apparently it is possible to cultivate such states of "lucid dreaming," as they are called, in which one is aware, while dreaming, that one is dreaming; and they can arise spontaneously as well. Such cases would fall under the same heading as things I can imagine while awake, that is, as imaginary in contrast to an external reality not subject to my will. Let's return, then, to the more problematic case of not being aware, while one is dreaming, that it is a dream, so that there is no sense at all of being in control of everything that is happening. One can dream of deciding on certain actions in the dream, but the important thing to notice is that this is against the background of what seems to be an external reality every bit as much as there normally seems to be an external reality while one is awake. So that it doesn't matter after all whether I am aware that I am dreaming. If I am, then I am also aware that it is only within the dream that I can make happen whatever I want. And if I'm not aware that I'm dreaming, then I am already seeing and feeling that there are things that I care about but can't control.

I can try to convince myself, intellectually, that for all I know, it could be that I'm really in control of everything that is happening now but that I am just unaware of it. But I guess I just don't really see the point of this. Could it be that I will be aware of it when all things are restored and God is all in all; that is, that since I will be one with God, I will be in control of everything, just as God is? But right now God chooses not to be in control of the things he leaves up to me, which include but are not limited to my ability to imagine whatever I want to imagine. That is, he could take away my freedom if he wanted to – as he does regarding those things that are not under my control – but evidently he does not want to. And when the ultimate goal is attained, everyone freely chooses to do God's will, and it is not a matter of God's forcing anyone to do so. Being in the right relationship with God doesn't mean being identical to God. "God is all in all" does not equal "God is all." It means that God is in control of the things he chooses to control, I am in control of the things he chooses to allow me to control, and I choose just as he would choose if he were in control, and likewise for everyone else.

This gives us something to go on in trying to answer the question, "What should I do now?" from the psychedelic Christian perspective. What it tells us is that first and foremost we should accept that there are important things that are not and never will be under our control. Even God doesn't choose to be in control of everything. After all, he leaves some things up to us. So why should we think we would want to be in control of everything? Our choice is whether or not to trust that this is the way things should be even when we would change things if we could. We may hope to act more and more according to God's will, but if we do, our acting that way is not what makes it God's will, and our willing it is not the same thing as God's willing it. Secondly, it is only because God has chosen to allow us freely to choose to do his will or not that we can do it. Otherwise, there would only be God, doing everything, and you and I wouldn't even exist.

Chapter Six

God's will and injustice

Marx thought that religion is the opium of the people because it mollifies the chafing of an unjust society by promising a non-material kingdom of God at some time in the indefinite future, while what is really needed is for the oppressed to seize political power and create a material heaven on earth in the here and now in the form of a communist society. What is right about this is that we shouldn't just shrug off injustice as something that only God can cure by imposing his will. God is never going to impose his will, except in the ways required for there to be a world with creatures who can freely choose to act justly or unjustly. Injustice ceases only when human beings freely choose to cease doing unjust things. What is wrong about it is that forcing someone to stop doing something unjust, which is all that political power can achieve, while often the right thing to do, can't prevent the injustice from springing up again as soon as the force is withdrawn, thus requiring a constant enforcement which will have the tendency to become itself a new form of injustice, so that those who were formerly oppressed become the new oppressors. And the more convinced the supposedly good people are that they are the good people and that if they can just succeed in forcing the evil people to quit being unjust all will be well, the more likely it is that the reasonable use of force to prevent injustice will itself turn into a new form of oppression, as I think history shows.

How do we bring it about that more and more people freely choose to cease doing unjust things? I think the place to start is to examine one's own motives and actions. In the Lord's Prayer we ask our Father in heaven to forgive us our trespasses as we forgive those who trespass against us. This links our awareness of our own acts of injustice with the willingness to forgive the unjust acts others have committed against us. How clear it is that sincerely and thoughtfully praying this prayer is to step in the direction of the cessation of injustice! If someone accuses me of committing an unjust act, my first reaction is to become indignant and to defend myself by denying to myself and to my accuser that I have done anything wrong. And sometimes I am right, and my accuser is wrong, and there is nothing more maddening than to be unjustly accused. In such a case, unless I can convince myself I never act unjustly, my prayer to God is that He forgive my injustices as I forgive the injustice now being committed against me. And if upon reflection the accusation turns out not to be entirely unjust, why then to that degree the act of which I was accused is one of those for which I am asking forgiveness.

When a scribe asked Jesus what the greatest commandment is, or what he should do to inherit eternal life, Jesus answered, "Thou shalt love the Lord thy God with all thy heart, and with all thy soul, and with all thy mind, and with all thy strength: this is the first commandment. And the second is like, namely this, Thou shalt love thy neighbor as thyself. There is no other commandment greater than these." (Mark 12: 28-31, also Matt. 22: 35-40, and Luke 10: 25-28) My gloss on this is that loving God with all your heart, and with all your soul, and with all your mind and with all your strength is believing, not just intellectually but also emotionally, experientially, bodily, that it is for the best that there are many events of life, both large and small, that are not under your control, and that there are others, both large and small, that are under your control. For example, you aren't in control of whether someone else chooses to act in a way that you believe to be in accord with justice, but you are in control of whether you act that way. That is the way it has been and the way it always will be. You may try to gain more control, and you may voluntarily give up some of your control;

and, depending on the situation, either of those may be the right thing to do or the wrong thing to do. But it will never be that you have no control over anything, and it will never be that you have control over everything. And you should be glad of that, because either of those alternatives would be the end of you. And you should think of whatever or whoever it is that makes you the person who you are – and not a mindless tool like a screwdriver or a computer whose sole purpose is to be used, nor a lonely god who controls everything only because nobody else exists as an independent person – you should think of that one who makes you the particular person who you are, in control of some things but not everything, as a loving parent, either father or mother, or sometimes one and sometimes the other. That is, what makes the world the way it is, is a person and not a thing or an impersonal force; because if it were a thing or a force, then you and I and everybody else would just be parts of that thing or masses of stuff subject to an external force, like dead leaves blown along by the wind. And we aren't like that. Being glad, you should be full of love. And, at every moment, you should love the next person to cross your path just as you love yourself. And this clearly implies that you should love yourself, and that he or she should love himself or herself. Because if you don't love yourself, then loving your neighbor as you love yourself would mean *not* loving your neighbor. This is why I think it is wrong to speak in terms of "transcending the ego." If all this means is that one shouldn't be selfish by acting as though nobody's interests count but one's own, then it is right. But it seems to suggest that the goal is to identify oneself as some sort of superior being who has no selfish interests, and I don't think that is either possible or desirable.

Why not? Because the only kind of being that has no selfish interests is an inferior sort of being: a thing or a force rather than a self. Yes, a loving parent may genuinely choose to sacrifice his or her life to save the life of his or her child. Jesus said,

"Greater love hath no man than this, that a man lay down his life for his friends" (John 15:13), and he did it. Soldiers have died by throwing themselves upon a grenade to save their friends, firefighters have lost their lives trying to save others, and mothers have died trying to save their children. But Jesus is our savior, and these people are heroes to us not because they were supposedly superior (really inferior) beings who had no desires of their own, but rather because their love was stronger than those desires.

Why does Jesus say that the commandment is to love your neighbor as yourself, that is, the one who is next to you, who is close to you? Why doesn't he say you should love everybody no matter how near or far? I think it is because the love that is commanded is concrete, particular, and precise. It is much easier to believe that one is obeying if one thinks the love that is commanded is abstract, general, and vague, flowing out from oneself to encompass all of humanity. But Jesus is saying I have to love this particular person I happen to be interacting with here and now, that is, someone who is much more likely than humanity in general to be thwarting my desires in some way, pursuing his or her own agenda, making demands on me, interrupting me, annoying me, not giving me the respect I so richly deserve. Humanity in general is so much nicer than that, never interrupts me, never disagrees with me, doesn't even seem to have an agenda of its own that could interfere with what I'm trying to do. True, in my mind's eye, I could look out over the billions of people who belong to humanity and imagine myself picking out first one and then another to be someone with whom I would interact here and now; but again it's probably easier to imagine loving that hypothetical neighbor than it is to love, really love, my actual neighbor as I love myself.

On the positive side of the imaginary versus actual contrast, though, it is also easier to justify to oneself hating an opponent whom one imagines than it is to justify hating one's actual opponent, face-to-face. It's harder to be completely blind to the fellow humanity of someone who is actually present with you than it is to neglect to imagine the fellow humanity of that ignorant, self-righteous, malicious and mediocre hypocrite, lying, incompetent hack whom you imagine when your opponent is only present in the form of some posting on the internet, or appearance in a news report, for example. I guess we should be glad we don't have to love our opponents as we imagine them. We only have to love them, as we love ourselves, when they happen to be, not "they", but this one, right here and now. Of course, that's hard enough, and, as I said before, as soon as we set an ideal for ourselves, we realize we don't meet it – at least not most of the time. But that is no reason to reject it as an ideal goal. If we had already attained it, it wouldn't be a goal. And that doesn't conflict with what I said before about the ultimate goal, that we have already attained it, and a new one is still coming. Assuming I do succeed in loving my neighbor as I love myself, there are always new neighbors to come.

* * *

If I love my neighbor as myself, I love him or her as having selfish interests of his or her own, just as I do. And yes, my neighbor's interests may at times come into conflict with mine. When they do, the goal is to effect some sort of reconciliation if possible or, if not, to accept the situation without viewing it as a cause to hate each other. After all, my own selfish interests also often come into conflict with each other, in which case, similarly, the goal is to figure out a way to reconcile them if possible or, if not, to accept the situation without taking it as a reason to hate myself. If I do hate myself, I inevitably end up hating my neighbor also. To the degree that a person can be justly criticized as selfish, to that same degree he or she has interests that conflict with each other but tries to be unaware of it and thus is unable to reconcile them or to accept the situation without hating himself or herself, and as a consequence, hates and envies others whom he or she perceives as undeservedly happy. The archetype or supreme degree of this is the Devil, who wants both to be God and to conquer God, and who thinks everyone else secretly harbors the same ambition. I suppose that if he could succeed in simultaneously being God and conquering God, he would have achieved that elusive goal of "transcending the ego."

Suppose the Devil is your neighbor. Does the commandment say that you should love him? And what would that mean? Here lurks a paradox. To the degree that you are a brother or a sister to the Devil, in that you, too, are unable to reconcile conflicts within yourself because you desire contradictory things, to that same degree you will hate yourself and hence hate your neighbor, who happens to be the Devil (we are supposing). But if you realize he is the Devil, you will also realize that in this regard, he is much worse off than you. Hence you will not envy him but rather pity him. But is pity love, or a form of love? Of course, there is the false pity of disguised conceit and condescension. No one wants that, but everyone wants to be loved. Still, I think genuine pity is at least a form of love. If I pity someone, I view him or her as a fellow sufferer. I understand the suffering of another if I have also suffered. And just as I want relief from my suffering, I want my fellow sufferers to be relieved also, and this caring is a form of love. Unamuno even thinks it is the deepest form of love, present in romantic love also, and I think he may be right. (*The Tragic Sense of Life,* Chap. IX)

So it is the very fact that the Devil is the supremely self-conflicted sinner that makes me pity and hence love him, because I too am a self-conflicted sinner but not as bad off as he is. So the paradox here is that one would think I should hate him because he personifies hatred and evil, but I should also love him, because he is my neighbor (we are supposing) and deserves my pity because he is so much worse off as a self-conflicted personification of hatred and evil than I am. But there is a deeper paradox, which is that in a way he plays a role similar to the one played by Jesus, who takes on all the sins of humanity and thereby redeems us from our slavery to sin and death. The difference is that the Devil intends to take us down with him but fails, while Jesus intends to release us and succeeds.

Chapter Seven

Release from sin and death

But what does it mean to say that Jesus releases us from sin and death? What connection is there between this traditional Christian belief and psychedelic experience? And what bearing does it have on the question of what we should do in light of the ultimate goal?

We are all sinners because Adam and Eve chose to disobey God's commandment not to eat of the fruit of the tree of the knowledge of good and evil. Objection: "Why should I be punished for what my first ancestors did? It isn't fair." But this very protest undermines itself. You wouldn't be complaining about this or anything else being unfair unless you, too, had eaten of the fruit of the tree of the knowledge of good and evil. You judge some things people do to be good and other things they do to be evil. You may not like to use the words "good" and "evil" and prefer to talk about "social justice," "human rights," "environmental justice," "racism," "sexism," "homophobia," "Islamophobia," and so forth; but the point is that you make moral judgments. Objection: "But why is that a sin? It's a good thing to care about social justice." Yes, well, given that people sometimes act unjustly, it is good to recognize injustice for what it is and to prefer that people act justly instead. The point of the Bible story, as I see it, is that sin enters the world at the very moment the ability to distinguish between good and evil enters the world. And I don't take the Bible to be saying it would have been better if this had never happened, because if it had never happened, the concept of "better" would have been empty. It would be like saying that it would be better if nothing was better than anything else. Before the temptation and the fall, during the creation, there is just the repeated statement, "and God saw that it was good," culminating at the end of Genesis 1 in these words, "And God saw everything that he had made, and, behold, it was very good." The tree of the knowledge of good and evil itself is good, as Gen. 2:9 makes clear: "And out of the ground made the Lord God to grow every tree that is pleasant to the sight, and good for food: the tree of life also in the midst of the garden, and the tree of knowledge of good and evil." But then in Gen. 2:17, God tells Adam, "But of the tree of the knowledge of good and evil, thou shalt not eat of it; for in the day that thou eatest thereof thou shalt surely die." Why did he warn against it even though he made it and it is good, and presumably its fruit is good also?

The prayer that Jesus taught his disciples to pray asks our Heavenly Father not to lead us into temptation but to deliver us from evil. But the Gospels tell us that before the beginning of his ministry Jesus was led by the Spirit to go into the wilderness for forty days and forty nights, where he was tempted by the Devil. (Matt. 4:1-13) And in the garden of Gethsemane, just before he is betrayed by Judas and seized by Roman soldiers, we find him praying, "Abba, Father, all things are possible unto thee; take away this cup from me; nevertheless not what I will, but what thou wilt." (Mark 14:36) In other words, he is praying that he not be tested and delivered to the evil ones. He is tempted to flee from the suffering he foresees, but he is willing to accept it if God wills it. And God does will that he be tested in this way and delivered to the evil ones. He does have to drink the cup so that "It is finished." (John 19:30) Similarly, God tested us humans in the beginning, by issuing his unexplained command not to eat of the fruit of the tree of the knowledge of good and evil. Adam's and Eve's failures to obey God's will led to the awakening of their moral conscience and hence of our moral conscience. We know we are sinners because we know we don't live up to our ideals, and we are punished by knowing that life is good and that we are going to die.

When a patriarch in the Old Testament dies, he is "gathered

to his people" (Gen. 25:8), or it is said that "he slept with his ancestors." (1 Kings 2:10, 15:8, 15:24, 22:50, 24:6, 2 Kings 13:13, 21:18, 2 Chronicles 14:1) Adam and Eve disobeyed God's unexplained and seemingly arbitrary command, and we feel that we would have done so also, even though obeying him would not have harmed us physically in any way and we were told that disobeying him would result in our death. We can easily imagine ourselves thinking as Adam and Eve must have thought: "The serpent makes sense. God didn't tell us why he didn't want us to eat the fruit of this tree because the real reason is that he wants to keep us ignorant. Surely, he wouldn't really kill us just for wanting to learn." Jesus obeys the will of God, even though it results in his being tortured and cruelly executed, and we feel that we would have acted like Peter, reflexively doing what it took to avoid the likelihood of the same fate. Adam and Eve at the moment of their temptation represent seeing ourselves as separated from God, so that we are envious of what God has and want it for ourselves. As a result of our envy, we think of ourselves as things that can be destroyed and lose consciousness forever. Jesus represents seeing ourselves as loving children of a loving parent, so that even when that which we most feared is actually happening, we are not destroyed but rise again. And we know good and evil, and we are better for it, because our faith is that the original goodness that God saw in his creation is still there, now suffused with the pity and love that makes us, not the playthings of the gods or the random outpourings of a self-generating machine, but rather the children of God. And this mother and father of us all doesn't just want us to lead an upright life above ground for around 100 years or, more likely, fewer, only to die utterly and forever. We do die, but we also have life everlasting.

And all of this is consistent with psychedelic experience, during which nothing is trivial but rather every little detail contributes to pattern upon pattern in an epic in which everything is at stake and reaches a peak or a depth that is a new beginning that turns out to be the continuation of one's life just as it was, but for the fact of all that one has just gone through.

Chapter Eight

The unforgivable sin

We are all sinners because there are always ideals we hold that we fail to live up to. Suppose someone denies this and claims not to have any ideals he or she has yet to live up to. I think we will find it difficult to believe this person. Objection: "But won't we finally live up to all our ideals when we reach the ultimate goal, and didn't you say we've already reached the ultimate goal?" Yes, but I also said there is always a new ultimate goal, and that means we discover new ideals we have not yet achieved.

We are all sinners and we are all forgiven for our sins. By the way, let me just say that I hate the bumper sticker that says, "Christians aren't perfect, just forgiven." I hate it because it implies that Christians are superior to non-Christians in that they are forgiven and non-Christians aren't, and this is not a bit less self-righteous than simply saying, "Christians are perfect. Non-Christians aren't." Non-Christians *are* forgiven too.

Jesus said that there is only one sin that is unforgivable: blaspheming against the Holy Spirit. And what is that? Well, it certainly isn't just not being a Christian. If it were, we would all be damned; because, even if a person is baptized in infancy and a Christian from that point on, she or he wouldn't have been a Christian before that; so, if not being a Christian was an unforgivable sin, all of us have committed it, and it would be the one sin that baptism can't wash away.

Given, then, that blasphemy against the Holy Spirit does not equal failure to be a Christian, what is it? The context in which Jesus proclaimed this to be the one and only unforgivable sin was one in which some scribes and Pharisees had accused him of driving out demons with the help of Beelzebul, the ruler of demons (Matt: 12:24-32, Mark 3:22-30) He had just been curing many people, including a man with a withered hand and another who was blind and mute, and he was being criticized for violating the Sabbath (curing the man with the withered hand on that day instead of insisting that he wait until the next day to be cured) and for using evil powers to rid people of their suffering. He responded with anger against the hard-heartedness of those who would have us believe that the commandment to rest on the Sabbath implies that no one should be healed on that day (Mark 3:1-6), and argued that if they really believed he was using the powers of demons to defeat demons, they should be glad, because that would mean Satan was defeating himself; and that if it wasn't by the power of Satan that he was able to heal people, then it must be by the power of God, so that they should see that the kingdom of God had come to them. It was at that point that he proclaimed that blasphemy against the Spirit will not be forgiven. (Matt. 12-25-31) So, blasphemy against the Holy Spirit is being so morally blind and confused as to be unable to see plain and evident goodness as goodness and instead to think that there must be something evil about it. It is unforgivable only because the intended recipient of the forgiveness would be unable to accept it, would think there is something evil about forgiving and being forgiven. If you are worried that you have committed this unforgivable sin, then you haven't, because your worry shows that you care about and can recognize goodness.

What this tells us about what we should do to reach the ultimate goal is that we should be open and ready to see goodness in the place where we find ourselves. If we can't do that, it won't help to be in the kingdom of heaven. No matter how bad you think you are, God forgives you and blesses you, but he can't accept and appreciate the forgiveness and blessings for you. Only you can do that for yourself.

We have already attained the ultimate goal, and we are reaching for a new ultimate goal. God forgives and blesses us, and we are still learning how true that is. How can I claim my psychedelic experience as evidence that we have already attained the ultimate goal? Did everyone freely choose to act justly during my peak experience? What I said before is that it is a matter of seeing that being in the right relationship with God is always there, underlying everything else that could be described as *not* being in the right relationship with God. Another way to put this is to say that whenever someone – I, you, or anybody else – is doing the wrong thing, is acting in a way that indicates not being in the right relationship with God, then he or she is, for one reason or another, deaf, dumb, and blind to the truth about the way things are. During the peak experience one sees, in a way that can't be put into words because it is too richly detailed and kaleidoscopically ever-changing but I will try anyway, that everyone, despite all her or his troubles that cause false steps resulting in being unfair to oneself and others, has moments of freely choosing goodness, with confidence, with no false steps, as sure as sure can be; and these moments, like this tremendous moment, are the true moments that constitute life in the kingdom of heaven. And we will all continue to enjoy such moments now and in a future that has no end. That part is guaranteed, but we can also hope, based on the faith kindled by such moments, that we will continue to act in such a way that the intervening moments of missteps and being out of the right relationship with God will become less frequent. How can we help each other to do that?

Chapter Nine

"My kingdom is not of this world."

When the ultimate goal is attained, no one acts unjustly towards anyone. How is that possible? Even people who love each other are sometimes unfair to each other. The solution is not to try to convince oneself that evil and injustice are illusions, so that in the kingdom of heaven the things which one now believes to be evil and unjust still occur but are no longer seen as evil and unjust. That could be true of some of our judgments but not all. Sometimes one is wrong in one's judgments, and something one thought was evil or unjust turns out to be good or just after all. But if we can't trust any of our judgments about good and evil, right and wrong, then we shouldn't trust the hope that the kingdom of heaven would be a solution either. So, it must be that in the kingdom of heaven the things you correctly perceive to be evil and unjust simply do not occur. No one does them. Anyone could, but no one does. And the reason no one does is not because of some external force preventing everyone from doing evil but rather because everyone loves the next one as him or herself.

If such a state is the ultimate goal, what can we do in the here and now to bring it closer? Obviously, we should choose and promote good things and doings and forgo evil ones. Understanding what is worthy of being chosen, and what isn't, is what ethics and moral discourse in general are all about. In light of what is reported in the gospels, Jesus thought that using parables, similes, and metaphors to convey what the kingdom of God is like was the best approach to persuading people to choose it. He also made it clear – and this is what I want to emphasize here – that **worldly politics will never lead to the kingdom of heaven.** This doesn't necessarily imply that worldly politics is one of the evil things that one should avoid. After all, a lot of activities that aren't necessarily evil are also unlikely to be the way, the truth, and the life – for example: sports, leisure and travel, fashion, career advancement. The difference is that few people confuse their interests in those areas with Christianity, while I'm afraid a great many people have a hard time distinguishing between Christianity and their political beliefs about how to make this world a better place.

The goal of politics is to create policies about how we live our lives together, where those policies are enforced by a system of rewards and punishments, with the emphasis on the latter. One might suppose that the more a political system relies on rewards rather than punishments, the better it would be, but then withholding a reward could be just as coercive as imposing a punishment. The important point is that if we take away the element of enforcement, if we're just talking about policies or, better, advice, that one is free to follow or not, then this is no longer politics we're talking about, but something else. That something else could be religion.

I'm not saying that what we do about politics doesn't matter. Political issues matter more than, for example, the successes or failures of athletes, whether in individual or team sports. But I am saying that politics doesn't matter in the way that religion matters. I think the more we treat politics like a sport and the less we treat it like a religion, the better off we are.

What makes following sports enjoyable is that it doesn't really matter who wins but we pretend that it does. And there are always more games, another season, another sport. Following politics can be enjoyable in much the same way. There are always day-to-day developments to follow, winners and losers, a side to root for. I'm not denying that political outcomes can affect our lives in more lasting ways than sports outcomes. Even so, I would argue that devoting one's attention to politics is no more directed towards our ultimate goal than is devoting one's attention to sports (or fashion, travel, or advancing one's career). And that is because our ultimate goal has nothing to do with forcing anyone to do anything, while politics has everything to do with forcing people to do things.

"But surely," one might object, "when it comes to politics it really does matter in terms of our ultimate goal who wins. After all, suppose some anti-religious party wins and makes it illegal to attend church and makes everybody profess atheism. Or suppose some supposedly religious party wins and imposes policies that follow from their distorted version of religion." My answer is that if that is true, i.e., that it really does matter in terms of our ultimate goal who wins politically, then all that matters is which side has managed to gain the controls that force people to act one way rather than another. And so, if that is true, then what we should hope is that God will settle things once and for all by forcing people to act in the right way. But God doesn't do that, though he could, and we shouldn't hope that he will, because if he did we would be machines rather than human beings; so that is not true. Worldly kingdoms, democracies or republics, constitutional monarchies, dictatorships, and oligarchies use force to make people obey the law. But Jesus said, "My kingdom is not of this world." (John 18:36) And so, by taking politics as seriously as religion, we are not going to help each other act in such a way as to make the intervening moments of missteps and being out of the right relationship with God become less frequent. How then? By being members of a church that reminds us of the moments of being in the right relationship with God and does not aspire to have political influence. It doesn't follow that, as citizens, we shouldn't participate in politics. It does follow that, as Christians, we should not believe that our political choices have anything to do with bringing us closer to the kingdom of God.

"So, are you claiming that using force to abolish slavery or to defeat the Nazis was wrong?" No, I'm not saying that. We should try to improve this world by political and military action when feasible. What we shouldn't do is to confuse this with the infinitely more important goal of being in the kingdom of heaven, where no one is forced to do anything and everyone freely chooses goodness every time.

Common sense morality tells us that one is morally justified in using force in self-defense and in defense of the innocent who are threatened by force. When I say that it was justified to use force to abolish slavery and to defeat the Nazis, I am applying this principle. Of course, the problem with this principle of common sense morality is that both sides in a disagreement about morality will claim and often sincerely believe that they are the innocent ones who are being threatened with force and thus deserve to defend themselves or to be defended by others with force. It doesn't follow that there is no objective right or wrong when it comes to applying this principle. If there were no objective truth about who really is the innocent party who deserves to be defended by force, then the disagreements would become purely a matter of each side asserting that it has the power to force the other to submit, and the issue would be decided whenever one side did in fact prevail over the other in terms of coercive force. It would be a consequence of such a view that what is really right or wrong about morality changes whenever the political or military situation changes. But claiming to be more powerful than someone else is clearly not the same as claiming to be more moral. So, we must conclude that there is objective truth about morality and that it is possible for the wrong side to prevail, and so disputes about the correct application of common sense morality cannot be resolved by force. All that is resolved by force is which side is more powerful. But this doesn't overthrow the principle that force is justified in self-defense when one is the innocent party and in defense of the innocent when they are victims of aggression. It just means the issue all hinges on who really is the innocent party and who is the aggressor in a particular set of circumstances.

When we have achieved the ultimate goal, none of this is necessary to say, because there aren't any aggressors. It is only during moments when we are falling short of the ultimate goal that this principle of common sense morality applies. It seems pretty obvious that applying it incorrectly, that is, getting it wrong about who really is the innocent party and who is the aggressor in any particular case, will not get us closer to the ultimate goal. And in any political controversy everyone thinks the other side is getting it wrong. The question is: will applying it correctly get us closer to the ultimate goal? Granted that sometimes we are unable to persuade someone that what he or she is doing is morally wrong and our choice is either to stand by thus allowing him or her to harm someone or to use force or the threat of force to prevent the harm, and that one or the other of these is the right thing to do in those particular circumstances; will doing the right thing bring us closer to the ultimate goal, where no such cases ever arise? I think the answer is that it will not. If the right choice is not to interfere, that will be because we foresee some consequence arising from interference that is worse than the harm we are allowing by not interfering. Nevertheless, we are choosing to allow that harm. And if the right choice is to intervene because there is no foreseeable consequence that is worse than the harm we choose to prevent, then we are preventing that harm only by using force or the threat of force. Either way, we have not made the kind of change that is required to move closer to the ultimate goal. That would only happen in a case where it is we ourselves who are the potential unjust aggressors, we come to realize it, and because of that realization, we freely choose not to commit that unjust act. But even this, also, is something one can get right or get wrong, and the plural "we" rather than the singular "I" allows for a typical kind of mistake here. That is, one can claim, "We are the aggressors here and we should stop our aggression," and mean, "You people are the aggressors here and you should stop your aggression," where one is addressing a faction within one's own party or a party within one's own nation whom one believes to be wrongfully using force or the threat of force under the name of the whole party or nation. In other words, one is really appealing to common sense morality or even threatening one's own use of force, in concert with other like-minded people, in the hope of getting other people to change their behavior. It's just that since these other people are ostensibly members of the same party or nation to which you belong, you can disguise your belief in your own personal innocence by saying, "We are in the wrong," while actually hoping to influence others to change their behavior and while you have no intention of changing your own. Again, that may be the right thing to do, but it won't bring us any closer to the kingdom of heaven. So, it is probably clearer to say that in regard to the threat or use of force the only right action that moves us closer to the ultimate goal occurs when an individual realizes that he or she is the unjust aggressor in a particular situation and thus chooses to change his or her behavior.

For example, I believe that those who argue that a woman has a right to choose to have an abortion because that decision affects only her own body are in grave error in denying that the fetus is an innocent party who has a right to life. Accordingly, I won't vote for politicians who support "a woman's right to choose" or whatever other euphemism may be used to name this immoral position, and I donate to organizations that work to change the law so that the fetus's right to life is legally protected. However, I don't think my beliefs and actions relating to this issue move us in the direction of the ultimate goal. What does move us in the right direction is any occasion in which a woman rejects the option of aborting her pregnancy, not because of any legal restrictions or fear of social disapproval, but simply because she loves the life growing inside her as a person at the beginning of a new life, who is as close to her in the present moment as anyone

51

can be – again, not because I or anyone else says she should but because she just does.

Another example is that we – Jews, Christians, Muslims, Hindus, Sikhs, Buddhists, Confucianists. Taoists, atheists, everybody – are justified in using force to defeat radical Muslims who seek to impose their religion by force, but we would be just as deluded as they are if we think doing so will move us towards the kingdom of heaven.

We need to make a distinction, then, between divine justice and worldly justice. God has the power to prevent everyone from ever acting unjustly, but he doesn't have the power to make everyone act justly as a consequence of love for him and for neighbor, since acting from love is not acting because one has been forced. However, he has the power to make us capable of loving him and our neighbor so that we always act justly; and we must assume either that he has exercised this power, so that we are responsible when we fail to use the capacity he has given us, or that he is responsible when we act unjustly. The kingdom of God happens when everyone exercises this capacity and loves God and neighbor so that everyone freely chooses always to do what is just as the natural consequence of that love.

Suppose our neighbor is acting unjustly and we have the power to make him or her stop, thus protecting the victim of the neighbor's injustice. We have tried persuading the neighbor, but it hasn't worked. In such a case, it would be just for us to force our neighbor to stop committing the injustice. Our love for our neighbor would prevent us from using any excessive force, but would not prevent us from using the force necessary to stop the harm to the neighbor's victim, unless using that force would result in greater harm than the harm prevented. So, we would be acting justly, consistently with love for our neighbor, for it is possible to love someone and also to force him or her to stop doing something unjust.

But would this action help bring about the kingdom of God?

We are assuming that refusing to take any action in such a case would not be the just thing for us to do, since it isn't just to allow preventable harm to someone when the prevention, as we are assuming, doesn't cause any equal or greater harm as a side effect. So, refusing to act would take us away from the kingdom of God. But would acting, so as to force our neighbor to cease acting unjustly, help bring about the kingdom of God, in which everyone always freely chooses to do the right thing, out of love? Maybe our forcing our neighbor to do the right thing would help him or her eventually to see the light? But in that case, why couldn't God simply force all of us to act in ways that would result in our eventually seeing the light, so that everyone would do the right thing out of love? And since that hasn't happened, why isn't God responsible for the unjust acts people commit against each other, just as we would be guilty if we chose not to intervene to prevent our neighbor from acting unjustly when we had the power to do so? Are we to say that God can't bring about his kingdom by a just use of force, but that we can? That hardly seems like piety. Surely it is more accurate to think that God can't do the logically impossible thing of bringing about love by using force and neither can we.

It follows that there is more than one way an act can be the right thing to do. The first and highest, the divine way is when the act is the result of love, not of being forced, and doesn't involve forcing anyone else to do anything either. That is the kind of act that is done in the kingdom of God, where everyone freely chooses to do what is right, out of love. The second, and not as high but still noble and virtuous in a worldly way, is when the act is the result of love, not of being forced, but does involve forcing someone else to do or stop doing something, and results in the prevention of injustice. Acts that are right in this secondary sense do not occur in the kingdom of God and do not help bring about the kingdom of God. If they did, God would do them all the time, and none of it would be any of our doing. And that is impossible, because in the kingdom of God, it is all our doing, as a result of exercising the capacity God gave us freely to choose to act in accordance with his will, out of love for him and for the neighbor. No one is forced by God or by anyone else.

To sum up, doing something unjust moves us away from the kingdom of God. Doing something just in the secondary or worldly sense leads us neither away from nor towards the kingdom of God. Doing something just in the highest and divine sense, that is from love, with no coercion on either side, moves us toward the kingdom of God.

Chapter Ten

Psychedelic Christianity and church

Would it be a good idea to form a new denomination, called Psychedelic Christianity, to help each other move closer to the ultimate goal? I tend to doubt it. I'm quite sure I don't have the talent for it, and I suspect that if other people did it, I would find something I didn't like about it. Psychedelic Christianity is just the religion of people who have had profound psychedelic experiences and believe that Christianity is the best religious expression of what they have experienced. We may be rare birds, but we exist. And I think it would be unchristian for us to try to flock together into a tiny denomination that would exclude our brothers and sisters who have no psychedelic experience and no desire to try it, for whatever reason. Like other Christians, we should just join whatever church we think tells the most truth.

But why join a church at all? Why not be spiritual but not religious? Doesn't organized religion have a bad history of religious wars and persecutions, and sexual and financial scandals? My answer is that, while we certainly want to avoid repeating the bad deeds done under the cover of religion, organized religion in general and Christianity in particular have contributed immeasurably to the rich treasure handed down to us by our ancestors. My own complaints against churches I've experienced in the past have been against the use of shame, fear, and guilt as tools to enforce social conformity, so that one does not feel free to express honest doubts. In fact, for most of my adult life, I have thought of myself as a believer in religious experience but not in God. It is only little by little over the past decade or so that my thinking has trended back towards theism, for the reasons I've expressed here: I have no control, and we humans collectively have no control, over things I and we care about very much; and yet I have faith that life is worth living and meaningful and that the universe with all its happenings is personal, and that there is an afterlife and a pre-life, which doesn't make this one any less important, although it does make me a little more relaxed.

Churches that encourage honest expressions of doubt and thoughtful enquiry into the richly symbolic language of the Bible are not as common as weeds, but they exist. The biggest problem I've found lately is that a church that initially seems very open and uninterested in enforcing a particular theological interpretation of the meaning of Christianity replaces the old social pressure to conform theologically with social pressure to conform in terms of political opinion, and feels compelled to take a purportedly "progressive" stand on all the hot-button "social justice" issues of the day. But since this "progressive" stance is believed to flow from Christianity properly understood, it turns out that such a church is just as rigidly dogmatic as any old-time "fundamentalist" one.

Not all theologically liberal churches are like that, but admittedly, depending on where you live, it may be hard to find one that isn't too rigidly dogmatic in either the old-fashioned "fundamentalist" sense or the modern "progressive" sense. In such a case, I'm afraid I don't have much good practical advice. Maybe it will help to remember that when the ultimate goal is achieved, everyone is a member of the church, and there is no coercion, overt or subtle.

It isn't that there should be no dogma at all, but just that it should be kept to the essential tenets of the faith. And it isn't that a Christian should have no political opinions, but I do think it is a mistake for a church to brand itself using political labels like "progressive" or "conservative," because that shows a fundamental misunderstanding of the teachings of Jesus, who said, "My kingdom is not of this world."

The light shed by awareness of the ultimate goal, then,

reveals that when it comes to politics, one should lighten up and always concentrate more on removing the beam from one's own eye than on complaining about the speck in someone else's. I'll admit that this is easier said than done.

Chapter Eleven

Psychedelic Christianity and Paul

When the ultimate goal is achieved everyone freely chooses to be fair and just, full of pity and love for the next person. Also, the world is more beautiful than one dared to expect, and the events of life are worthy of deep emotions. Appreciating the beauty of life in this world and expressing it through art are ways of moving towards the ultimate goal, which is just the supreme degree of this. Every little way in which one acts gracefully, appreciates the grace of others, and accepts the grace of God is a move towards the ultimate goal. As far as self-conscious practice is concerned, every effort should be directed towards an ultimately effortless grace. Those efforts themselves will be lovably awkward. It may be that the highest form of grace is to be lovably awkward. Maybe that is my best hope. And this is not limited to the pursuit of the fine arts. No matter what one's profession or calling, everyone's greatest work of art is the story of his or her life, told by living it. It is not lost in the light of the ultimate goal. It shines like gold in the light of the ultimate goal.

In the kingdom of heaven you are with people you love, and you like the people whom you encounter but don't yet know well enough to love. Also, you are at home, or if you are traveling, either you feel at home wherever you are or you can return home whenever you wish. But is there no excitement, no thrill of risk? It may be that you must risk everything to enter the kingdom of heaven – Jesus' words and example seem to say so – but is there any danger in staying there, or is there a risk that, once there, you will leave? Judging from psychedelic experience, I would say there is a place of absolute safety from which you can venture out with the risk of not being able to find your way back and even of forgetting, temporarily, that it is there, but with the assurance that eventually you will remember and find your way back. In the meantime, your actual family, friends, and home are the entrance, the way forward, to the ultimate goal.

"That sounds nice, but then why did Jesus say, 'Whoever comes to me and does not hate father and mother, wife and children, brothers and sisters, yes, and even life itself, cannot be my disciple. Whoever does not carry the cross and follow me cannot be my disciple' (Luke 14:25-27)?"

As best as I can understand, Jesus is warning us against thinking that we are satisfied with something short of the ultimate goal. I love my father and mother, wife and children, brother and sister, and I love life; but I must admit that at times I have hated or at least failed to love each of these, even if only momentarily. If I am not honest with myself and fool myself into thinking that the love I feel now is so strong that it excludes the possibility of hate, then I will think I can do without the love that really does exclude the possibility of hate and the life that doesn't end with a fatal illness or wound. Clinging to this life doesn't work. If you think that either you have what you have in this life or you have nothing, you cannot really enjoy this life. That is why Paul said, "If for this life only we have hope in Christ, we are of all people most to be pitied." (1 Cor. 15:19)

There are those who would like to de-emphasize Paul's contributions to Christianity by concentrating on the quotations that can be attributed to the historical Jesus according to scholarly standards. I think that this is at least sometimes motivated by a disagreement with some of the things Paul said about the role of women in the church and about the sinfulness of homosexuality. My own views are: 1) that there is no more a general reason for women to obey their husbands than there is for men to obey their wives; and earthly obedience isn't "where it's at" anyway; and 2) that we have no good reason to think that sex between two men or between two women is any more likely to be ungodly than is sex between a man and a woman. So, if Paul disagrees with those claims, and it appears that he does, then I think he is wrong about that. But this doesn't take away from the depth and beauty and truth of his vision of our being children of God, who die with Christ and are resurrected with Christ. He wrote, for example,

> "So do not lose heart. Even though our outer nature is wasting away, our inner nature is being renewed day by day. For this slight momentary affliction is preparing us for an eternal weight of glory beyond all measure, because we look not at what can be seen but at what cannot be seen; for what can be seen is temporary, but what cannot be seen is eternal." (2 Cor. 4:16-18)

What can be seen is the outside. What can't be seen is the inside. But the inside is experienced, directly, by each one of us. Psychedelic Christianity is based on the empirical principle: try it and find out for yourself. It is a distortion of empiricism to think of it as belief in only what can be confirmed by what appears to the senses, or else we must expand our concept of "the senses." If I feel joy, for example, is that something I know through sense experience? Out of all the people I know about, I know which one I am. Is that something I know through sense experience? Whose sense experience? Empiricists prefer belief in what is experienced by oneself directly over belief based on someone else's claim to authority. Ironically, all too often people who think of themselves as believers in science betray empiricism by accepting unquestioningly the pronouncements of authority figures who claim to speak for science. If we are to accept a claim as based on scientific research, we must understand the claim and at least something about the research. Of course, we don't always have the time or the desire to look into it for ourselves, and so we accept the word of someone whom we regard as an honest expert. But we at least have to do a little thinking about whether there are other credible experts who disagree and about criteria for deciding who is more likely to be reliable. Otherwise, our acceptance of a supposed authority's claim is worthless.

Similar considerations apply to supposed religious authorities. Psychedelic Christianity is not an appeal to the Bible as "the inerrant word of God." The appeal is always and only to what rings true in the light of one's own experience. This doesn't mean that we should never rely on authorities or that we shouldn't regard the Bible as authoritative. It just means that there is no escaping the fact that one has a choice as to whether or not to believe a particular source is a reliable authority; that when one does rely on an authority, one can only really do that by understanding what the authority says as it applies to one's own experience; and that accepting that a person is an authority doesn't necessarily imply that everything he or she says is correct. So, I don't think it is unchristian to accept the Bible as an authority and yet to reject its condemnation of homosexuality, just as we disagree with its failure to condemn slavery (Exod. 21, Deut. 15:12-15, Eph. 6:5-8, Col. 4:1) and its prescriptions of rituals, sacrifices, and penalties in Leviticus.

Chapter Twelve

Forgivable sins

The one unforgivable sin is failure to accept and appreciate goodness. What are the sins which are forgivable, the ones, as we are told, for which Jesus died in order to save us from what we dread the most? What are our trespasses for which we pray to be forgiven? The Lord's Prayer compares them to those committed against us and which we pray also that we forgive; so, thinking of the trespasses committed against us should help us generalize about the trespasses we ourselves commit. For example, the trespasses against us that we most resent and find hardest to forgive are of the same type we should be most worried about committing ourselves. And it might be more helpful to think about what trespasses against us have in common rather than to compile a list. To one degree or another, what a person resents is being treated with contempt, as if one is of no importance, has no interests worthy of being taken into account, is not worthy of respect as being a separate person but is rather more like an object to be used for whatever purposes the other person desires, or simply to be discarded like trash. And the extreme of this, the contempt of indifference, is the opposite of being loved, which means that hate is not the opposite of love and not what we resent the most, for we don't really hate things – at least not as much as we can hate other people. Cold indifference is the opposite of love. Of course, we would prefer to be respected than to be treated like an object, but we would prefer even more to be respected and loved, and when we get respect without love, we still feel at least slightly sinned against, since being loved is the opposite of being treated like something that can be either used or discarded like trash, whereas being respected isn't. After all, someone can respect the power of something useful, as long as it is useful, only to discard it later when it ceases to be useful. But we know our usefulness to others in this life is limited, so we want others to consider us not just as useful, but lovable whether we are useful or not. When people fail to treat us this way, we feel we have been trespassed against, that to some degree we have been treated like an object and not a person. We find it hard to forgive this, even though we know we ourselves don't always find everybody we encounter to be lovable but often think of them as obstacles or as tools for furthering our own interests.

If we think of a mother and a father loving their baby, one thing that is pretty clear is that it isn't because the baby has done anything to earn it. After all, being cute is not something that is done to earn love, and we usually regard someone who thinks he or she is cute, and therefore deserves to be loved, as obnoxious rather than lovable. And yet to some degree we're all like that. We want to be loved just for being ourselves, but very often we don't find ourselves loving everybody else just for being herself or himself. In other words we think we're cute enough to be loved by everyone, but not everyone is cute enough to be loved by us. And that is our sin. How does Jesus save us from it? His parables indicate that in the kingdom of God each person is loved one-on-one in a way that no one could have earned and that has nothing to do with utilitarian considerations about how this affects anyone else. This means that even though our thinking we are cute enough to be loved by everyone does not make us lovable to each other, in God's eyes we are about as capable of being unlovable as a kitten or puppy, and God will never discard us or allow us to be discarded like trash. This is proved by the fact that when the Jewish high priests and the Roman authorities decided it would suit their purposes to have Jesus crucified, he was resurrected into life everlasting. And Jesus himself is the one who tells us God will do no less for us.

We should give up on trying to be lovable to everyone, but we shouldn't go the other way and try to demand respect by showing how formidably dangerous we are. Pilate reminded Jesus that he, Pilate, had the power to release him or to have him crucified, and Jesus replied, "You would have no power over me unless it had been given to you from above...." (John 19:10-11)

We often fail to forgive those who trespass against us, and God loves us anyway. But when we do forgive those who trespass against us, we are acting in a way that shows we understand and appreciate this, and that moves us in the direction of the ultimate goal.

What I have just said seems to imply that God doesn't take seriously any way in which we trespass against him. But there is that one unforgivable sin of not accepting the goodness that is freely offered. And the divine goodness is not the kind that can be spoiled by remembering that we also suffer disease, injury, and death. When Jesus says that in order to follow him we should take up our cross, I think he means that we should face it that life does involve suffering and dying. But his promise of the coming of the kingdom of God and his resurrection show that in the face of suffering and death we have eternal life in a world that redeems all suffering.

It is probably an oversimplification but may be helpful anyway to say that not accepting the goodness that God offers, trespassing against him in a way he takes seriously for our sakes, comes in three varieties: 1) the despairing intellectual type, in which one believes there is no ultimate solution to suffering and death but only temporary distraction; 2) the satisfied pagan, or effectively distracted, variety, in which one may profess a religion but doesn't take it too seriously and devotes oneself to either wealth and fame or to respectability; or 3) the political religionist form, in which one is either a conservative who behaves as though political enforcement of traditional values is the ultimate goal or a progressive who behaves as though the ultimate goal is political enforcement of social justice and scientific progress. The blasphemer of the third type may or may not claim to be a Christian. What constitutes the sin is treating the political goal, whether it is protecting traditional values or achieving social justice and scientific progress, as supremely important, as if having the correct political view is the way to salvation. The blasphemer of this type who claims to be a Christian will think that the political goal is implied by the teachings of Christ.

As I said before, since I don't see how the restoration of all things and God being all in all is compatible with there being people who are never redeemed, I think the unforgivable sin is unforgivable only while it is being committed, in that refusing to accept goodness and forgiveness is all that is blocking them. So, I think even the unforgivable sin of blaspheming against the Holy Spirit, i.e., refusing to see the good in something that is manifestly good, will be forgiven as soon as one stops committing it. Still, during the time that it's unforgivable, it's unforgivable. Jesus was exasperated with the Sadducees, scribes, and Pharisees, when they acted as though they lacked ears to hear and eyes to see. And he said that it is easier for a camel to pass through the eye of a needle than it is for a rich man to enter the kingdom of heaven, and I think that is because a rich man acts as if he believes that his wealth can save him from death. But when Jesus was asked by his disciples, "Then who can be saved?" he replied, "For mortals it is impossible, but for God all things are possible," and promised "the renewal of all things." He said, "But many who are first will be last, and the last will be first." He didn't say those who will be last won't be there at all. (Matt. 19:25-30) That is why I think those who commit the unforgivable sin won't keep on forever doing so, and that they will be forgiven and also will enter the kingdom of heaven, or realize at last that they already have.

In the meantime and to remind myself, I say: if you are a despairing intellectual, I dare you to take 250 micrograms of LSD. (But first read pp. 82-93 of *Dreams and Resurrection*.) Why not? What do you have to lose? You claim that life is meaningless anyway. If you are a satisfied pagan, I dare you to imagine that you have just been informed by your doctor that you have a terminal disease. Why not? It has happened to plenty of people, and it could happen to you, too. Anyway, we all die of something eventually, and you know very well that your wealth, fame, or respectability is no cure. If you are a political religionist of the conservative type, I dare you to explain why it is all right for you and people who agree with you to try to impose what you think are the correct moral and religious values and practices on everybody by force, in light of the fact that God could easily do that if he wanted to but evidently doesn't want to. Or do you think God is doing it through you and your political allies when he didn't do it through Jesus? If you are a political religionist of the progressive defender of social justice and science type, I dare you to answer the same question I posed to the conservative political religionist. I also ask you to imagine that your political activism and defense of science have succeeded beyond your wildest dreams, so that everyone would flourish under a just and prosperous political system, medical science would cure every disease and successfully treat every wound, and migration to other planets would solve the resulting overpopulation problem. Wouldn't it remain true that everyone who had suffered and died before the achievement of the political and technological utopia would still be as dead as ever? Surely it would be unjust that they would be left out simply because they had been born too early. And can you be sure that your political enemies, who had unsuccessfully opposed your noble efforts to achieve a just and prosperous society, would harbor no grudges about having been forced to go along? Do you hope some great mind would invent a technology that would bring back to life those who had died in the past, as the very same individuals who they were? Do you hope a political system would not require the enforcement of any laws? Why then, you are not a political religionist after all. You are hoping for the kingdom of God just as much as I am, and not as something that we humans as we now are could ever bring about on our own.

From the Wikipedia article on "The Social Gospel":

"Theologically, the Social Gospellers sought to operationalize the Lord's Prayer (Matthew 6:10): 'Thy kingdom come, Thy will be done on earth as it is in heaven.' They typically were post-millennialist; that is, they believed the Second Coming could not happen until humankind rid itself of social evils by human effort."

But this is clearly contrary to what Jesus taught as represented in the Gospels – and what better source do we have about what Jesus taught? Jesus didn't predict that social justice would be achieved before the coming of the Son of Man. Instead, he predicted wars and rumors of wars, earthquakes, famines, and much suffering in general. (Mark 13:8) And it is a misinterpretation of the Lord's Prayer to think that it is a prayer for human precepts about how to rid the world of social evils to be put into practice. Jesus' promise is divine justice, not social justice. Everyone will be restored to life, free of suffering from natural afflictions. Neither will anyone suffer from unjust acts committed by other humans, but this will not be because the "good people" have used military force, political power, or social pressure to make the "bad people" behave. It will be because everyone freely chooses to do God's will, from love of God and neighbor. When John the Baptist, from prison, instructed his followers to ask Jesus, "Are you the one who is to come, or are we to wait for another?" Jesus didn't answer by citing any kind of political or social progress he had accomplished. He said, "Go and tell John what you hear and see: the blind receive their sight, the lame walk, the lepers are cleansed, the deaf hear, the dead are raised, and the poor have good news brought to them. And blessed is anyone who takes no offense at me." (Matt. 11:2-6) He didn't "speak truth to power." When he was being questioned by Caiaphas and Pilate, he didn't defend himself. When he "told off" the scribes and Pharisees, he did it to teach the others, who had ears to hear and eyes to see. He wasn't interested in political power. He told Pilate, "My kingdom is not from this world. If my kingdom were from this world, my followers would be fighting to keep me from being handed over to the Jews." (John 18:16) He didn't seek political power or encourage his followers to do so; instead, he exhibited power, miraculous power. He didn't say we should do better in applying common sense morality. He said we must be more righteous than the Pharisees, that we must be perfect as our Father is perfect, that we must take up our cross; but all of this, he promises, is easy and light, and we should not let our hearts be troubled. Jesus said, "For to those who have, more will be given, and they will have an abundance; but from those who have nothing, even what they have will be taken away." (Matt. 13:12) As social justice this makes no sense, and of course neither is it meant to justify rich people making themselves richer at poor people's expense. It makes sense only as divine justice about having or not having faith. At Matt. 15: 8-9, Jesus quotes Isaiah:

'This people honors me with their lips,
But their hearts are far from me;
in vain do they worship me,
teaching human precepts as doctrines.'

Chapter Thirteen

The Holy Spirit

The Holy Spirit comes down to you, or wells up within you. This is not something that you can make happen, but you can be on the watch for it. You may do something or stop doing something because of it, but nothing you do or stop doing is the cause of it. It is being supplied constantly, but only sometimes are you receptive of it. The inspiration and creation of art is an example of what I mean. When you are moved by listening to a beautiful piece of music, or by reading a great work of literature, or by gazing at a beautiful drawing or painting or statue, you also may be moved to admiration of the composer, writer, or artist who created it, as well you should be; but you should also reflect that your appreciation of the beauty of that work of art is something to which you have opened yourself. It was already there. You just didn't pay attention to it before. It is something that is happening to you at least as much as it is something you are doing. After all, you know very well you didn't compose it, write it, draw or paint it, or sculpt it. But likewise, for the composer, writer, draftsman, painter, or sculptor, it is also true that the creation of the work of art was at least as much something that was happening to him or her as it was something he or she was doing. The entire process of inspiration-execution-appreciation is the goal of art. The Holy Spirit inspires the artistic execution, which in turn inspires the appreciation of the listener, reader, or viewer. The artist doesn't create the inspiration of the Holy Spirit any more than the listener, reader, or viewer creates the execution of the work of art by the artist. The goal of life is a similar process of inspiration-execution-appreciation, where, perfectly receptive to the inspiration of the Holy Spirit, you express it with all your heart, and with all your soul and with all your strength and with all your mind; and so does everyone else, and we all enjoy each other's way of doing it.

When we reach for the ultimate goal, we are reaching for new eyes, new ears, a new tongue, a new nose, new hands, new genitals, new arms and legs, a new heart, lungs, brain, guts, skin, hair, bones, blood and muscles; and yet also in another way, the ones we've had all along; to see, hear, taste, smell, touch, all the shapes, edges, colors, movements, sounds, smells, flavors, textures; to lust, to walk, to breathe, to fear, to grieve, to talk, to read, to think, to love, to eat and drink, to suffer, to pity, to hurt, to help; to move towards a new ultimate goal as glorious as this one, and as glorious as those of the past whose autumnal fading into wintry quiet were folded within this one and now unfold again like the leafy buds and flowers of spring into the full bloom of high summer.

We do this to experience a new world with each other, or the same dear old one in a new way. "This world" always just means the one we're in, and any others will always be imaginary. But everything we imagine, everything we fear or hope for, dream or remember, also belongs to this world. When we are in the kingdom of heaven, this world is the kingdom of heaven. *We have already achieved the ultimate goal*. It is finished. We are saved. This world is the kingdom of heaven. *There is more than one ultimate goal*. The enjoyment of the kingdom of heaven by each one of us is as ultimate as it gets. God is our God only if we are there to enjoy his being all in all. *There is always a new ultimate goal*. We are always forgetting and always remembering. It is still coming again. God bless you, dear Reader, God bless you.

References

Bergson, Henri. *Creative Evolution*. Mitchell, Arthur, trans. Mineola, NY: Dover Publications, Inc., 1998.

Bultmann, Rudolf. *Jesus Christ and Mythology*. New York: Charles Scribner's Sons, 1958.

Call, Jack. *God is a Symbol of Something True: why you don't have to choose either a literal creator or a blind, indifferent universe*. Winchester, UK, and Washington, DC, U.S.A.: Circle Books, 2009.

___ . *Dreams and Resurrection: On Immortal Selves, Psychedelics, and Christianity*. Winchester, UK, and Washington, DC, U.S.A.: Christian Alternative, 2014.

Pascal, Blaise. *Pensées and Other Writings*. Levi, Honor, trans. Oxford: Oxford University Press, 2008.

Santayana, George. *The Sense of Beauty*. New York: Dover Publications, 1955.

Schelling, F.W.J. *The Ages of the World*. Worth, Jason M., trans. Albany: State University of New York Press, 2000.

___ . *Bruno or On the Natural and Divine Principle of Things*. Caterer, Michael G., ed. and trans. Albany: State University of New York Press, 1984.

___ . *Clara or, On Nature's Connection to the Spirit World*. Steinkamp, Fiona, trans. Albany: State University of New York Press, 2002.

de Senancour, Etienne Pivert. *Obermann*. Barnes, J. Anthony, trans. Baltimore: Noumena Press, 2010.

de Unamuno, Miguel. *Selected Works of Miguel de Unamuno, Vol. 5: The Agony of Christianity and Essays on Faith*. Kerrigan, Anthony, trans. Princeton: Princeton University Press, 1974.

___ . *Tragic Sense of Life*. Crawford Flitch, J.E., trans. New York: Dover Publications, Inc., 1954.

From the author: Thank you for reading *Psychedelic Christianity.* I hope you enjoyed reading it as much as I enjoyed writing it. If you have a few moments to add your review of the book at your favorite online bookseller, I would be very grateful. Also, if you would like to connect with other books I have coming in the near future, please visit the website of the Institute for the Advancement of Psychedelic Christianity for news on upcoming works and recent blog posts. http://myiapc.com

CHRISTIAN
ALTERNATIVE

Christian Alternative

THE NEW OPEN SPACES

Throughout the two thousand years of Christian tradition there
have been, and still are, groups and individuals that exist in
the margins and upon the edge of faith. But in Christianity's
contrapuntal history it has often been these outcasts and
pioneers that have forged contemporary orthodoxy out
of former radicalism as belief evolves to engage with and
encompass the ever-changing social and scientific realities. Real
faith lies not in the comfortable certainties of the Orthodox,
but somewhere in a half-glimpsed hinterland on the dirt track
to Emmaus, where the Death of God meets the Resurrection,
where the supernatural Christ meets the historical Jesus,
and where the revolution liberates both the oppressed and
the oppressors.

Welcome to Christian Alternative... a space at the edge where
the light shines through.
If you have enjoyed this book, why not tell other readers by
posting a review on your preferred book site.

Christian Atheist

Belonging without Believing

Brian Mountford

Christian Atheists don't believe in God but miss him: especially the transcendent beauty of his music, language, ethics, and community.

Paperback: 978-1-84694-439-0 ebook: 978-1-84694-929-6

Compassion Or Apocalypse?

A Comprehensible Guide to the Thoughts of René Girard

James Warren

How René Girard changes the way we think about God and the Bible, and its relevance for our apocalypse-threatened world.

Paperback: 978-1-78279-073-0 ebook: 978-1-78279-072-3

Diary Of A Gay Priest

The Tightrope Walker

Rev. Dr. Malcolm Johnson

Full of anecdotes and amusing stories, but the Church is still a dangerous place for a gay priest.

Paperback: 978-1-78279-002-0 ebook: 978-1-78099-999-9

Do You Need God?

Exploring Different Paths to Spirituality Even For Atheists

Rory J.Q. Barnes

An unbiased guide to the building blocks of spiritual belief.

Paperback: 978-1-78279-380-9 ebook: 978-1-78279-379-3

The Gay Gospels

Good News for Lesbian, Gay, Bisexual, and Transgendered People

Keith Sharpe

This book refutes the idea that the Bible is homophobic and makes visible the gay lives and validated homoerotic

experience to be found in it.
Paperback: 978-1-84694-548-9 ebook: 978-1-78099-063-7

The Illusion of "Truth"
The Real Jesus Behind the Grand Myth
Thomas Nehrer
Nehrer, uniquely aware of Reality's integrated flow, elucidates
Jesus' penetrating, often mystifying insights – exposing
widespread religious, scholarly and skeptical fallacy.
Paperback: 978-1-78279-548-3 ebook: 978-1-78279-551-3

Do We Need God to be Good?
An Anthropologist Considers the Evidence
C.R. Hallpike
What anthropology shows us about the delusions of New
Atheism and Humanism.
Paperback: 978-1-78535-217-1 ebook: 978-1-78535-218-8

Fingerprints of Fire, Footprints of Peace
A Spiritual Manifesto from a Jesus Perspective
Noel Moules
Christian spirituality with attitude. Fourteen provocative
pictures, from Radical Mystic to Messianic Anarchist, that
explore identity, destiny, values and activism.
Paperback: 978-1-84694-612-7 ebook: 978-1-78099-903-6

Readers of ebooks can buy or view any of these bestsellers by clicking on the live link in the title. Most titles are published in paperback and as an ebook. Paperbacks are available in traditional bookshops. Both print and ebook formats are available online.

Find more titles and sign up to our readers' newsletter at
http://www.johnhuntpublishing.com/christianity
Follow us on Facebook at
https://www.facebook.com/ChristianAlternative